Traci S'teele

30 Day MAN Cleanse

The guide to keeping your sanity with men!

Traci Steele

ISBN-13: 978-1986278102
ISBN-10: 1986278107

Copyright © 2018 Traci Steele
All rights reserved.

DEDICATION

I want to dedicate this book to all the men in my past who didn't treat me right. I had to go through a few assholes to push me to write this book and to turn to God. I want to thank my best friend Marquetta for giving me the idea to cleanse. Thank you to my mom Averil, for giving me life and showing me what a female boss represents. Thank you to my aunt, Dorrett for always being there. Thank you to my family and friends for supporting my vision. Most of all, thank you to my handsome, funny, intelligent son Andrew for giving me purpose and showing me unconditional love. I will never love anyone more than you.

CONTENTS

Day	1	Purge
Day	2	God Hears You
Day	3	Reflect His Love
Day	4	His Will
Day	5	Close Doors
Day	6	Patience
Day	7	Signs From God
Day	8	God's Strength
Day	9	Love Again
Day	10	Trials and Tribulations
Day	11	Cheerful Heart
Day	12	You Will Not Fall
Day	13	I Am What I Am
Day	14	The Truth Will Set You Free
Day	15	Temptation
Day	16	Healing A Broken Heart
Day	17	Confess Your Sins
Day	18	Be Still
Day	19	Loving Again
Day	20	Love Never Fails
Day	21	God's Time
Day	22	Inner Peace
Day	23	Forgiveness
Day	24	Gratitude
Day	25	Seek God First
Day	26	Sex
Day	27	Friendship
Day	28	Prosper
Day	29	Prayer
Day	30	End Of The Cleanse

ACKNOWLEDGMENTS

The inspiration for this book was given to me by my Lord and Savior I acknowledge You, praise You and give You the glory!

I should start with the truth about why I decided to write this book, The 30-Day Man Cleanse. First, I'm a woman who is passionate, which can be confused with crazy. I honestly hate when a woman is titled crazy after she reacts to a man who plays with her emotions, ruins her mental health, gave her reason to act out, and even if it's justified, he calls her crazy. I won't claim the word crazy, but I will fight for anyone I love. I curse like a sailor. I'm loud, blunt, and I'm way too honest. Yup, I am one of those chicks and because of my prominent personality people automatically assume that I am not as spiritual as I am; but the saying "Don't judge a book by its cover," is exceptionally accurate when it comes to me. I'm literally on the cover of this book, and by looking at me, you wouldn't know anything about my spirituality other than she's cute. I certainly don't dress like a nun, and I act like I should have been arrested more times than I have. Don't judge me; I'm just being honest. Even though I can be extra, which is not easy to deal with at times, I still wholeheartedly and with every breath in my body believe and trust in God. I pray to God every single day and one of the things I've prayed for desperately was my soul mate, my other half, my future husband. Jesus, where is he? Why is he taking so long to come? Will I ever get married? Somehow, with all that praying, I am still alone. My past relationships have been one train wreck after the another. It started with a broken heart from my son's father, Andrew. He cheated while I was pregnant and I thought I would never move on from that. It hurt so badly that I didn't want to live anymore. Imagine being in so much pain that someone else put you through and from that pain, you'd want to take your own life. That was the hardest pain I had endured. However, with time I became more and more numb to heartbreak. Don't get me wrong it still hurts but not as much as the first time. (Sigh) Sad but I have managed to move on, praise God and now Andrew and I are great friends, and he is a phenomenal father.

After Andrew I fell into a pattern or type of men I seem to always meet. They were all narcissists with commitment phobias and substance abuse issues. Just writing this makes me feel like I'm completely screwed up but the first step to dating recovery is knowing the problem. My next heartbreak was someone who I knew was wrong for me but I thought I could change him. There was no changing LePreston. He dragged me through hell then blamed me for why HELL was so hot.

The relationship wasn't that long, but the love was so profound and so intense that when he finally left, I felt like I got hit by a car, a small car, maybe a scooter, but it still hurt none the less. I fell hard for LePreston because he was the most affectionate man I had ever met. Imagine someone loving you every moment that he is with you. I even adored the taste of his skin. He was everything to me, and in the beginning, I felt protected. He looked at me like I was the only woman in the world. He touched me every chance he could, and he was good at making me feel like I was his everything. I distinctly remember when we use to shower together, he would hover over me so manly and strong, and all I felt was love. LePreston for a moment made me feel like the happiest girl in the world but with the good came the evil. I started calling him the devil at one point, so when he left, I was relieved. He was both physically and verbally abusive. That was the first and last time I will ever be in a relationship like that. Wait, I forgot to mention he had an addiction to pills and women. He seems to fall in love quicker than usual. He said, "I love you" after two weeks and forced me to say it back. He wanted me to save him in a sense. He wanted me to get pregnant so that he could lock me down, and he wanted me to help him with his career. He fell in love with anyone woman who could help him. He also had violent mood swings which resembled signs of bipolar disorder. Now, I am not a psychologist, but when I see him screaming, crying, kicking in my door, and threating to kill me because HE CHEATED, there is something incredibly wrong. I tried to help him with his dying rapper career and all I got in return was a bloody lip and dragged down the steps in my house by my hair. I also have horror stories about him going through withdrawals, but I'll keep the gruesome details to myself and get to why I stayed with him as long as I did. First, for selfish reasons, I thought we looked good together walking on a red carpet and secondly, I thought I could change him. That's most women's downfall, assuming they can help or improve a man. After LePreston, I dated and hung out with comedians, basketball players, rappers, Hollywood stars and reality stars. Which led to why I wrote this book. I started dating someone in the spotlight and for all intents and purposes he was utterly wrong for me. However, his charisma, mogul qualities, and masculinity took my breath away. Just in case you're wondering, how was the sex? I wasn't hooked on his dick. It was too big for me which is not a compliment. It wasn't pleasurable. It was actually painful most of the time. What made me bond with him was his extreme affection. For that very reason, I kept going back. His love for his kids also drew me in and to this day he gives the best head known to man. That tongue is made of diamonds and pearls lol, but I digress. All his best qualities had me to the point where I knew I could love him despite what ALL my friends said about him. My friends honestly thought because of his reputation for being a player, that he was beneath me and I could do so much better. The relationship was short-lived. Steven drove me crazy to the point where I needed a break from ALL MEN. Steven possessed traits of a typical narcissist, which I didn't know much about at the time that we dated. He lacked empathy; he was selfish, self-absorbed, and unable to understand what I was feeling. Narcissists expect others to think and feel the same as they do and seldom give any thought to how others feel. They are also rarely apologetic, remorseful, or accept guilt.

I had to look up what a narcissist was because I had never met a man like Steven. It was and still is hard for me to believe people like this exist and can function in life. Dealing with him was impossible, no matter how I expressed my emotions he would completely ignore my feelings. Steven just doesn't notice or even care what anyone else is feeling. To make it worse to shut me up he'll just get me whatever I wanted. Seriously, anything I wanted was mine. He gave gifts to pacify me for the time being but that didn't fix the problem. I never in my entire life met a man who didn't care about your point of view at all. He never asked simple questions like, "How was your day?" "How are you feeling?" "What are you doing?" You know why he never asked because he didn't care. However, he had no qualms sharing his whole existence with me. Whether I asked or not. He might as well have dated himself since he was the only one that mattered in the relationship. At that point, I decided I couldn't take it anymore, and I needed to do something because these men had me ready to jump off a very high sidewalk… lol, seriously I felt confused, low, and lost when it came to relationships. Really, why is it so complicated? It can't be this damn hard! I had so many questions, I know I'm a good woman, I don't just come to the table, I bring the whole damn table, why won't he treat me right?

Why doesn't he listen? Does he even care? Why the hell won't he act right?

That's when I turned to my best friend, Marquetta Breslin. I just wanted to vent about my relationship problems, but she said, "what you really need is a break!" Take a 30-day man break and take that time to reconnect with God and with yourself. In all honesty, I said to her, "Bitch, I've been single for YEARS how much more of a break do I need ??!!" Quet said, "that was not a real break, you still dated, talked to, and occasionally slept with men, and that needs to stop for 30 days". The whole concept was foreign and mind-blowing at the same time. I never heard about this type of break from men but I was excited to try it out. How do I just stop altogether? No calls, no texts, no direct messages, no communication whatsoever with men I'm dating, talking to, or interested in. No cut buddy, also known as friends with benefits, it all just stops! Can I let them know I'm not talking to them? How is this going to work?

From there I started writing scriptures every day and posting them on my Instagram story @TraciSteele and then the light bulb came on! I got an epiphany. The idea for this book came, and I started writing immediately. I thought if I stayed away from men completely, no calls, no text, no direct messages on social media, no booty calls; and focused on prayer, meditation, and me, that God would lead me down the right relationship path. After 30 days, I will be closer to God and can see the signs better with no distractions, i.e., men. I'm not saying after 30 days you will find your soulmate. I'm saying after 30 days, you will see yourself, know what you want, and have a distinct understanding of what you deserve. All while growing your relationship with God that you will need so you receive signs when the Devil sends you a soul mate in disguise. You're taking the 30 days to love yourself more than a man. Once you truly love yourself and build that connection with God, you'll know when it's time to let go. You'll have a clear mind and heart to hear God when He shows you the signs to move on or if that man is the one. Let's be honest here, there is nothing wrong with taking time for yourself just to better yourself. When I posted on my Instagram that I am man cleansing for 30 days, the comments were all similar. Women were saying, "I have been cleansing for years," which is hard to believe. Just because your single for years doesn't mean you've been on a cleanse for years. Just being single is not a cleanse. The cleanse includes NO COMMUNICATION, whatsoever and daily prayer. Again, this is only men you're dating, interested in, seeing, in love with, or screwing. It even includes that old raggedy baby daddy, ex-husband, or ex-boyfriend that wants you back. If you have a child with the man you need to cleanse from, you'll have to find a way to co-parent without communication which means you get a family member or friend to relay messages for 30 days. If your kid has a phone even better, they can call their dad whenever they want to be picked up or dropped off. Now, let's say you're messing with a co-worker and you have to find a way not to communicate. My suggestion is talk only about work and after work, they are cut off.

Realistically, you know you need these 30 days because these men have been pushing you to throw hot grits on their ass while they sleep. Ok, maybe that's just me lol. During this cleanse you will have moments of weakness and moments when you really, really want to reach out to him. The problem is as you're going through this cleanse your emotions and feelings will get in the way of you being great. You will have moments, which was every single day for me, where you want to say what's on your mind at that very moment. Even if it's to say "you ain't shit !" You have to remain strong. Trust me you always think it's super easy from day one. Then day nine hits and you think you're going to give up. Complete and utter lack of communication with a man is unnatural to me and the statement "you want what you can't have," really kicks in during this cleanse. Oh, what I would give right now for a sexy ass man to whisper," I missed you" in my ear but I can't. I am writing this book as I cleanse, and even though I want to text or call him so badly, I won't. I know at the end of this I will be better off. I know I can take these 30 days with no distractions to figure out whatever is in my heart with God guiding me instead of my emotions or my vagina making the decisions.

Now let me tell you something, I have friends who have said to me that they can't move on from someone so wrong for them because of the sex. I've heard it all, "he's the best I ever had," "how can I do better?" "He makes me cum multiple times, and no one else does that." "He has the biggest appendage I've ever seen, who can top that?" In my opinion SEX is the most significant manipulation mechanism ever created. You can hate a man and still have sex with him because it's good. But it doesn't fix the problem. It only further bonds you to that man. By the way, if you didn't know, when a woman orgasms, her body lets off a hormone called oxytocin which bonds you to the man. Women produce more of this hormone. Although it's not apparent why, and this means they are more likely to let their guard down and fall in love with a man after sex. However, the problem is that the body can't distinguish whether the person we're with is a casual fling or marriage material. Oxytocin releases either way. So, while it might help you bond with the love of your life, it's also the reason you may feel so miserable when you're hooked on someone so entirely wrong for you.

Man! It's not easy being a woman, you have so many distractions that can guide you down the wrong path. Sometimes the answer is right in front of you. But you're blinded by love, sex, or the feeling of loneliness. The thing with feelings is it has a quiet way of sneaking up on you when you least expect it and next thing you know you're hooked on his ass. Do you know how insane it feels to bond with the wrong person? To love or care about someone who treats you like shit? All you want is happiness, and the men in your life consistently bring you stress and sleepless nights. So, are you feeling like you need this man cleanse now more than ever? What would you do for peace of mind?

For the next 30 days, you will pray. You may cry then pray some more, and ask God to show you. After

30 days, I want you to come out of this cleanse stronger and more resilient when it comes to men, relationships, and life in general. This process is about self-discovery and spiritual enlightenment. Life is too precious for you to be feeling anything but happiness. Life is too priceless for you to be feeling anything but love, so take this 30-day journey so you can reignite your faith and gain self-acceptance as well as let go of all the things that hold you back. The cleanse is relatively simple, yet it tests your willpower, focus, and strength all at once. Every day for 30 days you will read the scripture out loud. Internalize it then get on your knees and pray. Let's start!

Traci Steele

Day 1

***"Create in me a clean heart, O God, and renew a steadfast spirit within me."* (Psalm 51:10)**

If you're reading this book, it's not by chance. God wants you to know Him and to hear Him. He wants you to renew your faith and to grow in the Holy Spirit, but you cannot build with dead weight attached to you. You have to get rid of the weight to flourish. You have to purge! First, you should know what purge means. It's to free (someone) of an unwanted feeling, memory, or condition. Typically giving a sense of liberating release. Once you choose to purge or release what is toxic in your life, you can then begin to focus on yourself and what you need. You can build back your self-esteem and self-love. So, for this particular cleanse let's start with purging out your phone. Go through your phone and start deleting old contacts, old lovers, old boyfriends, and block anyone who takes you out of your peace. With no interference, the next 30 days is about you connecting to yourself and God!

Today's Prayer:

"Father God, thank You for allowing me to see another day. I ask that You renew me and forgive me for any errors in the past. Let me try again to walk closer to Your will. I acknowledge I cannot make it without You. Walk with me and show me Your way. Uplift my heart and allow me to rekindle my faith. In Jesus name, I pray, Amen."

Day 2

***"This is the confidence we have in approaching God: that if we ask anything according to his will, he hears us." *(1 John 5:14)**

We are praying for the next 30 days because God enjoys answering our prayers. As we seek God through reading the Bible and prayer, we gain wisdom and spiritual insight. Giving us a greater understanding of His will for us. God answers every prayer that aligns with his will. On the flipside, James 4:3 "When you ask, you do not receive because you ask with the wrong motives It's not about using blessing for your pleasures." This verse from the book of James tells us why God says *"No"* to many of our prayers. They may be selfish, self-centered, or even bad for us. God will say no to our prayers if we ask for something for the wrong reason or if it's not of His will. So today, pray selflessly and with an open heart. Ask Him to remove anyone in the way of His calling for you.

Today's Prayer:

"Father God, You have so much more in store for me. Help me make room for all of Your blessings in my thinking. Give me the strength to stay focused on this 30-day cleanse. Show me how to live with faith according to Your word. Continue to lead me to do better through failure and success. Guide my decisions with Your ultimate knowledge and remind me that Your way is best. In Jesus name, I pray, Amen."

Day 3

"Love the Lord your God with all your heart and with all your mind and with all your strength. The second is this: Love your neighbor as yourself. There is no commandment greater than these." **(Mark 12:30-31)**

Life is not about your accomplishments, popularity, or prestige. It's about how well we love. One eye-opening reason that keeps us from loving fully as God intended is the more disconnected we are, the more fearful we become. What I mean by disconnected is we are so busy checking e-mails, texting and social media that we are not talking to each other anymore. If we are doing everything except talking how do we establish a deep connection with anyone? Not only that, we crave intimacy, but we fear vulnerability. We want love, but we're scared to give 100%. So, the question remains, how well do you love? Do you love with conditions and hesitation? Do you love with a wall up? Do you let your past affect how you love now? Today, take a few minutes to meditate on this scripture and ask the Lord to show you how you can reflect His love to others in your life.

Today's Prayer:

"Lord, let me love unconditionally as You love me. Help me forgive without holding on to anger and disappointment and let me be kind and forgiving as You have forgiven me. Please guide my thoughts, heart, and action, so my life is a testament to You. May Your love, peace, joy, and patience reside in my heart. In Jesus name, I pray, Amen."

Traci Steele

Day 4

***"In the same way, the Spirit helps us in our weakness. We do not know what we ought to pray for, but the Spirit himself intercedes for us through wordless groans."* (Romans 8:26)**

If you cannot pray and leave the answering of that prayer to the Father, accepting whatever He chooses to send as His will in that situation, you quit praying. If you pray and there isn't an immediate answer, or you don't get what you want you just might quit praying. God has His plans. He wants our faith in Him to be unwavering. Just trust that God is at work this very moment. Do not be surprised if God's answer to your prayers is not what you asked or wanted or expected. But what you said you wanted above all was His will to be done. Today, ask the Lord to help you walk by faith and believe in His will.

Today's Prayer:

"Father God, thank you for the blessings I understand and the ones I don't. Thank you for the miracles I see and the ones I don't. Let me be ok with this day no matter what it brings. For everything that's in my life and everything that's not. I trust that You already know what I need and are manifesting my prayers this very minute. In Jesus name, I pray, Amen."

Day 5

"Those who hope in the Lord will renew their strength. They will soar on wings like eagles; they will run and not grow weary, they will walk and not be faint." (Isaiah 40:31 NIV)

When it comes to relationships, how many times have you said, "I'm done!" "I'm not going back!" "It's over!" Then you went back, you called, you texted, knowing it's not the right thing to do. That happens more often than none. It sometimes feels impossible to find your strength to stay away. Especially when you have a bond or love for this person; there's so much you want to say; so much to get off your chest. You know in your heart nothing you say is going to help because you said it all before but you pour out your heart anyway and get ignored or they just plainly don't care. It hurts you to your core that they won't change or won't stop hurting you but really, it's you that has to make the change. You have to find the strength to walk away. Trust me, walking away has nothing to do with weakness and everything to do with strength. You walk away, not because you want others to realize your worth and value, but because you finally realized your worth and value. To build your strength, you need to put your trust and hope in God. Get your power renewed with consistent prayer, fellowship, and worship. It's the Word of God that will build you up even at your weakest point. Pray today that God gives you the strength to close old doors to open new blessings!

Today's Prayer:

"Heavenly Father, I trust You to open the right doors in my life and shut the wrong ones. Even when I don't know what to do; I have faith that I can hear from You and follow Your lead. Thank you for giving me the power to close a door that will ultimately reveal a blessing. I need You. I need Your holy spirit to give me strength. In Jesus name, Amen."

Traci Steele

Day 6

"You also must be patient. Keep your hopes high, for the day of the Lord's coming is near." (James 5:8)

Have you ever thought, when is it my turn? How long am I going to be alone? Lord, I'm not getting any younger, why is it taking so long? The cliché, "patience is a virtue," is annoyingly frustrating, BUT it is undeniably true. Patience is talked about throughout the Bible in the Old and New Testaments. According to 1 Samuel "lack of patience can cause you to miss blessings," and Paul lists patience in Galatians 5:22-23 as among the "Fruit of the Spirit." The problem is we live in times where everything is instant. People want everything NOW. So developing patience can be difficult. Keep reminding yourself over and over again that it is God's plan not yours. "Be still before the Lord and wait patiently for him." (Psalm 37:7). When loneliness tests our patients, it is our mighty and loving God who will, in time, lift our sadness. He will give us the patience to wait for what is better for us and what is God's will. Wait on Him!

Today's Prayer:

"Father God, we live in a culture where people want everything and wants it now. Help me to break free from these ways and replace this restlessness with calm and peace. Help me make room for all of your blessings in my thinking. Show me how to live with expectancy according to your word. Jesus, I ask that you grant me patience and allow the holy spirit to be my guide and lead me to do better through failure and success. Lord, thank you for providing for the needs I have now and for the blessing that is yet to come. In Jesus name, I pray, Amen."

Traci Steele

Day 7

"So, Jesus said to him, "Unless you people see signs and wonders, you simply will not believe." (John 4:48)

Have you ever felt like something is just not right in your relationship or while dating? It may be a gut feeling or a feeling of uneasiness. This discomfort just might be a sign from God. He is trying to get your attention. God may speak to us softly during prayer or scream from the rooftops trying to get us to notice Him. On the flip side, God might make you feel that something is just not right and you have no sense of peace. There is a feeling of overall uneasiness in your life. Let me help you even further. Here are some clear indications that God is trying to get your attention. Physical, mental or emotional exhaustion; harmful or hurtful people leaving your life; the feeling of being lost or purposeless; an opportunity to go on a long trip or retreat; the awareness that you've been repeating the same relationship mistakes for years or persistent frustration and lack of peace. Now raise your hand if one or more of these indications are happening in your life. Not all of God's signs are enjoyable, some are unpleasant and painful, but how else are you going to listen to God when he says "WAIT!" Today, ask God to show you a clear sign so you can continue on the right path that He has set for you!

Today's Prayer:

"Heavenly father, so often I ignore you, disobey you or challenge you, yet you keep on showing and teaching me the right way to live. Help me to see your will for my life. Let your spirit guide my words and deeds. Lead me to always to give you praise. I will trust you and believe your word that assures me. In Jesus name, I pray, Amen."

Traci Steele

Day 8

***"I can do all things through Him who strengthens me."* (Philippians 4:13 NIV)**

I love this verse. Write this verse on your mirror in your bathroom. You need to see it every morning so it can boost your spirit. This verse will help you take on the day. It's like a victory chant. It makes you feel powerful knowing that you can do anything through God. No matter what circumstance comes your way, you will prevail. Say this every morning to keep you steady through this 30-day journey.

Today's Prayer:

"Lord, give me the strength You've promised in Your word. Give me the courage and the power to conquer whatever comes my way. Give me grace and even in my weakest moments, reveal Your strength. Into Your hands I place my worries, cares, and troubles; and into Your love, I place my life. In Jesus name, I pray, Amen."

Day 9

"Love is patient and kind; love does not envy or boast; it is not arrogant or rude. It does not insist on its way; it is not irritable or resentful; it does not rejoice at wrongdoing but rejoices with the truth. Love bears all things, believes all things, hopes all things, endures all things." **(1 Corinthians 13:4-7)**

Go back and read that scripture again. Now think about it. Can you honestly say you have had that type of love? In this verse, Paul begins to paint a picture of love's qualities. In this beautiful description of the nature and effects of love, it is meant to show the Corinthians that their conduct had, in many respects, been a contrast to it. If you read that scripture a few times you will realize the love you've received in your life has felt like a hot mess yet, you still crave love. You may have trouble defining it, explaining it, and even finding it, but you know deep down inside that we need it. Today, I want you to identify the love you are seeking. Be specific and ask God for exactly what you want. The scripture is clear. You can see this love displayed in patience, kindness, humility, forgiveness, integrity, and ongoing perseverance. This kind of love survives and stands the tests of time even through hardship. Ask God to open your heart so you can give and receive the love you want and deserve.

Today's Prayer:

"Father God, remove any anger and contentment from my heart that prevents me from loving those deserving of it. Let me love unconditionally as You love me. Help me not to bring past issues into the present so that I hold no grudges. May Your love, peace, joy, and patience reside in my heart, in Jesus name, I pray, Amen."

Traci Steele

Day 10

***"So that the proof of your faith, being more precious than gold which is perishable, even though tested by fire, may be found to result in praise and glory and honor at the revelation of Jesus Christ."* (1 Peter 1:7)**

This scripture is about trials and tribulations and the test of your faith. I'm here to tell you that during this 30-day cleanse you will be tested to see if you can make it through. You can fulfill your promise to yourself and God with your daily prayers with no distractions. Are you going to give in? Are you going to fail? The test can come in any form, and it is meant to throw you off course. It can be as simple as a text from your ex or as hard as him showing up at your door. You have to stay strong to pass the test. Today, tell God you will make it through to the end and praise him for the strength to do so.

Today's Prayer:

"Thank you, Lord, for the merciful things You have done and are doing in my life; even in the midst of trials and tribulations, You show me favor. Lord, help me prevail on the journey of spiritual growth and oneness with you. Let no one divert me from my ultimate goal of knowing myself and knowing You. Continue to move mountains and guide me towards my destiny. In Jesus name, Amen."

Day 11

"A cheerful heart is good medicine, but a broken spirit saps a person's strength." **(Proverbs 17:22)**

No truer words were ever spoken! In a relationship when you are happy, flowers are prettier, the sun shines brighter, the colors are more vivid, but when the relationship is tumultuous oh, how it shifts. It can take you to a dark place. A broken heart or spirit can leave you feeling desolate and damaged. You barely want to get out of bed in the morning, much less go to work with a broken spirit. Unfortunately, a bad relationship can indeed break your spirit, and it's up to you to get your strength back. Today, pray for a cheerful heart, for joy, for peace for happiness so that you can rejoice every day with God's mercy!

Today's Prayer:

"Heavenly Father, forgive me for complaining. I have been going through a tough time, and I need You more than ever. Help me to see that Your plan is greater than my struggles. I know that You have put me in my current situation for a purpose. I believe Your plan to help me to grow into the strong person You want me to be. Give me the spirit of gratefulness, joy, peace, and clarity. Help me to find happiness in You alone. Lord, I desire to have a heart that seeks You and no one else. In Jesus Name, I pray, Amen."

Day 12

"God is within her; she will not fall."
(Psalm 46:5)

Typically, in life, there are highs and lows. The lows seem like you are being beaten up or beat down. For me, my lows drain me. I feel tired. I'm tired of struggling, tired of not winning, tired of waking up and going to sleep then doing it all over again. Most of all I'm tired of doing this all by myself, with no companion, soul mate or husband. When you start to feel this way, you need to repeat this verse out loud. Speak it so that God can hear you, "God is within me, I will not fail!" This verse is powerful because it speaks to women who need reassurance that as long as you trust in Him, you will make it through stronger than ever. Put your trust in God, and he will lead you through any situation, circumstance, or a problematic relationship. You will not fall if you let God lead. Be obedient because He is not just beside us or around us, but within us. Today, rise and declare his enduring power over you.

Today's Prayer:

"Father God, I will let no one discourage me from being the leader you made me to be. You know every decision I need to make, and every challenge I face. I know I can overcome anything because I trust in You. Lord, I ask that You lift my spirit, lift my finances, lift my health and lift my relationships. I need

Your holy spirit to give me strength, wisdom, and directions. Amen."

Traci Steele

Day 13

"By the grace of God, I am what I am." (1 Corinthians 25:10)

Sometimes in relationships, you lose yourself. You can love someone so much that you don't even see yourself anymore. You just see what they want. You put their feelings first. You help build them up and you spend a lot of time thinking about their needs or happiness before your own. The next thing you know you have cleaned up this man, helped him with his career, given him swag; and all that time and attention you gave him could have been spent developing yourself. You helped him build his empire and forgot about your own. You helped him fulfill his dreams, but what about your own? In the next 30 days, you will focus on you for a change. You will figure out who you are today and who you want to be in the future. Your first, last, and best love is self-love. So, take the next 30 days to pamper and take care of yourself. Set goals for yourself, create your vision board and think only about your next step. Today, tell God I am not perfect. I am going to make mistakes, so I ask that you watch over me. Guard me so that I can walk the path you have for me. Help me to fall in love with myself again because I am who I am!

Today's Prayer:

"Heavenly Father, continue to encourage me and help me to focus on my calling. Help me to trust your power instead of my plan. You forgive me, and you see the best in me even when I don't see it in myself. Defend me against temptation. Help me to see the examples of your unfailing love so that I can love myself as you love me, Amen."

Day 14

"And you will know the truth, and the truth will set you free." (John 8:32)

"You" in this scripture refers to those who are faithful disciples of Jesus. True disciples will know the truth. More than that, their eyes are opened to a greater understanding of the truth. The truth Jesus's disciples receive, brings with it freedom. With the truth, you can free yourself, yet some of you know the truth, and you still stay. You know he's wrong for you. You know he hurts you. You know it's a chaotic relationship, and you always stay or take him back. Your feeling of peace is gone. Your relationship feels like it's in turmoil. You know it's because of the man you can't seem to shake. Your mind always seems to wander back to him. You try to find reasons why you want him in your life. However, you know he doesn't treat you the way you deserve. He has done you dirty numerous times and numerous times you cave and let him back in. Before the truth can set you free, you need to recognize that the lies are holding you hostage. Today, ask God to expand your thoughts and beliefs on which that is true, for God is the only source of truth. As you spend time communicating with God, ask Him to show you and guide you to the truth and to freedom.

Today's Prayer:

"Lord our God, may you reveal what is hidden and bring to light what is in the dark. Reveal all that needs to be revealed. You can do all things even things beyond my understanding. Help me to focus on Your word which is a truth that sets me free. I enter this day with faith knowing You will show me the way to be free and be at peace. I trust You, and I believe Your power and spirit will take possession of my life, Amen."

Traci Steele

Day 15

"Keep watch and pray, so that you will not give in to temptation. For the spirit is willing, but the body is weak." (Mark 14:38, NLT)

If you have been spiritual for more than a day, you probably know what it means to be tempted by sin. Resisting the urge to sin is difficult on your own, but when you turn to God for help, he will empower you with wisdom and strength to overcome even the most enticing temptations. Walking away from things we know are not healthy for us becomes easier and more comfortable. When we tap into God's power through prayer we can resist the lure of temptation with his words of truth in scriptures. If you are facing temptation right now, get encouragement by praying this prayer and standing your ground with reassuring Bible verses. In the next 30 days, the temptation can be as simple as you wanting to reach out to that guy or him trying to connect with you. Today, pray that God helps you resist temptation.

Today's Prayer:

"Heavenly father, you know my heart. You know that I stumble and sometimes fall but right now I need your help. I am being tempted. I admit my weaknesses and vulnerabilities and I ask that you guide me through. My spirit is willing, but my flesh is weak. Lord, strengthen me with the shield of your word, Amen."

Day 16

***"He heals the brokenhearted and binds up their wounds."* (Psalm 147:3)**

No one ever goes into a relationship thinking they are going to get their heart broken if that were the case there would be no relationship. Unfortunately, out of a relationship can come a broken heart, which at that moment feels devastating. Why are breakups so excruciating? Is it because everything reminds you of them and hence the loss of a relationship? Music, a smell, a place, your first "I love you," can all bring back unwanted memories. Immediately after a breakup, it is difficult going 24 hours without bursting into tears. Love can feel like a drug, and after a break up you feel like an addict going through withdrawals. Going through withdrawals from a man sounds insane. Wondering if you're addicted is not the real question. The question is how do you move on? I can tell you what heals all wounds: time and prayer. I know you don't want to hear this because you want to stop hurting now, and stop thinking about them now. There is no instant fix for a broken heart. When you're feeling lost or at your lowest, lift your spirit by repeating this verse to yourself. Know that He will heal your broken heart. The Lord above has the power to remove all hurt, anger, loneliness, and struggle. Let Him take away your pain through prayer, worship, and faith. God can and will redeem your broken heart. Have faith you will feel His peace within you again soon. The ending of a relationship is never painless, mainly when you're always thinking about your ex. A tough breakup can consume your life. Today, ask the Lord to guide you through these difficult times. To help you find peace in your heart, ask God!

Today's Prayer:

"Lord, I try hard not to stumble in my walk of faith, but You know the heartache that I face. Sometimes the pain and hurt seem unbearable. I need Your help to get through this painful time so that I can come out stronger than I was before. I cannot walk alone. I need your guidance. Lord, the trials, and griefs I suffer cannot compare to the glory that awaits me. I ask You, Lord, to heal my heart, heal my emotions and heal my spirit. In Jesus name, Amen."

Traci Steele

Day 17

"If we confess our sins, He is faithful and righteous to forgive us our sins and to cleanse us from all unrighteousness." (1 John 1:9)

These 30 days are primarily a spiritual detox. It's 30 days of reflections and renewal. To do that we need to confess our sins to God and ask for forgiveness. You need to cleanse yourself of shame and regret, fear and worry, selfishness, bitterness, envy, habits of sin, negativity, doubt, procrastination, and laziness. Research has shown that it can take as little as 21 days of doing something consistently to develop a habit. With that being said after this 30-day cleanse, you should be in the habit of praising God daily, loving yourself, feeling joyful, confident, and filled with positivity. What is so spectacular about the cleansing is that these acts are in absolute harmony with God's purpose. The Lord wants us to live an unbelievably blessed life through Him. Don't let negativity and sin hinder those blessings. Today, ask God to cleanse you and forgive you of your sins. You accept the sacrifice Jesus made on the cross and will follow and obey Gods will.

Today's Prayer:

"Lord, I am thankful beyond words for Your sacrifice. Help me serve You, obey You, follow You, and please forgive all my sins. I trust in the sacrifice Jesus made on the cross. I know You are working every little detail of my life out and that I have nothing to fear or worry about because You protect me. Create in me a clean heart, so that I can follow the path that is in line with Your word, Amen."

Traci Steele

Day 18

"Be still and know that I am God."
(Psalms 46:10)

Sometimes we can't sense God's presence because there's too much of everything else going on at once. There's too much noise, too much traffic, too much confusion, too many thoughts running rampant in our minds, and too much anxiety. When this happens, I wish I could unscrew my head and put it down somewhere just to get a moment of peace. Sometimes it feels like your mind is the enemy. You just can't stop thinking, worrying, stressing, but there is a way to get that stillness: prayer. Center your mind on Him and start to breathe deeply. Try it. Exhale the distracting thoughts. Inhale a desire to sense His presence. Exhale your daily stresses. Inhale a desire to know Him more completely. Exhale the worries of the moment. Inhale His peace. Now, don't you feel better already? Can you begin to sense Him?

Today Prayer:

"Oh Lord, You know my heart, You know my struggle and You hold each hope and fear in Your caring hands. Teach me, Lord, to be still in the midst of the storm, for Your timing is always perfect. Lord, I desire to hear You and seek You about all else. In Jesus name, I pray, Amen."

Day 19

***"Get rid of all bitterness, rage, and anger, brawling and slander, along with every form of malice. Be kind and compassionate to one another, forgiving each other, just as in Christ God forgave you."* (Ephesians 4:31-32)**

When someone hurts you, especially someone you deeply loved, the thought of forgiveness is the last thing on your mind. It can be one of the hardest things we face in life! The pain and hurt others cause you are real and significant. It's extreme and sometimes overwhelming, but the pain of living with bitterness and un-forgiveness can poison your soul and devastate you. When you forgive others, you are not saying what they did was OK, but you are releasing them to God and letting go of its hold on you.

Today's Prayer:

"Dear Lord, I thank you for the power of forgiveness, and I choose to forgive everyone who has hurt me. Help me to release any pain or animosity so I can walk in righteousness, peace, and joy. I choose to be kind and compassionate, forgiving others, just as You forgave me. With gratitude, I can draw closer to you and let go of any negativity. With gratitude, I can see the person who caused my pain and pray for them with love and acceptance. Help me find the compassion that comes with true forgiveness. In Jesus name, Amen."

Day 20

"Love never gives up, never loses faith, is always hopeful, and endures through every circumstance." (1 Corinthians 13:7)

We talked about heartbreak already; now I want to talk about loving again. After a breakup some people stop believing in love or the feeling of the breakup was so overwhelming they just don't want to love again. In 1 Corinthians 13, Paul will argue that love is an action, not an emotion. With that, over the course of the last 20 days, our consistent reaction was to be thankful as we pray. Our action was to grow closer to God and build a stronger spiritual connection. I think we can agree that our actions show our love for God and that is the right step to loving others. You can and will love again but first, let's learn to love ourselves and our Lord and Savior.

Today's Prayer:

"Lord, thank you for loving me first. Help me know You more and love You more. Help me demonstrate unconditional love today, even to those who hurt me. Help me release the hurt and begin to love as Jesus loves. Help me to enhance my bond with You so that I can open my heart to Your blessings. In Jesus name, I pray, Amen."

Day 21

"There is a time for everything and a season for every activity under the heavens." **(Ecclesiastes 3:1)**

If you've ever taken a long road trip with friends or kids, there's a 99.9% chance that you will hear someone in the car say "are we there yet?" Even though there is a long journey ahead, people tend to want to hurry things up. When times are going great, we seldom ask, "How much longer is this going to last?" But, when times are rough; they seem to go on for eternity. I can admit it can be hard to trust God's timing. It looks as if we are not even on God's clock. There is never a time in which He is not aware of the desires of our hearts. He does, however, know better than we do, whether what we want to happen, is necessary or even useful for us. Throughout your life, there will be plenty of moments when you wish things would move along a little quicker. Perhaps we are in a difficult season, and we just want it to be over as soon as possible. Though it is natural to want to look ahead, we run the risk of missing the things God needs us to see at this time and in this moment. He is not ignoring us when time seems to stand still, but rather keeping us in the present so we may prepare for the upcoming future. Today, pray for the acceptance to trust God's time.

Today's Prayer:

"Heavenly Father, You know every decision I need to make and every challenge I face. Please forgive me for the times that I tried to figure this life out on my own. I need You. I need Your holy spirit, Your glory, and Your mercy. Open my eyes to see that your time is the best time for me. Cast out fear, remove all doubt, block disbelief, and cause an unwavering trust to stir within me. In Jesus name, Amen."

Traci Steele

Day 22

"You teach us to let the peace that comes from Christ rule in our hearts." (Col. 3:15)

The Hebrew word for peace is "shalom." It means completeness, wholeness, and contentment. Who in their right mind wouldn't want wholeness and contentment? But how easy is it to find peace in your heart and your life? Life feels like an insane roller-coaster with the most amazing highs and the most staggering lows, so where does peace fit into this equation! Knowing peace is understanding how it has nothing to do with control. You can't control the personal hardships you will face in life. Your circumstances affect your mental state, but they don't have to control them. Admittedly, it's not easy to choose peace when we're going through tough times, but there are countless things we can do to create peace of mind. You can meditate, communicate, connect with others, stay active, but for me the best path to peace of mind is prayer. So today, ask God for peace of mind and grant a clarity of thought to feel at ease in your life.

Today's Prayer:
"Lord, please calm my fears, soothe my anxious soul, release my anger, and help me to let go all frustration. Keep me complete and whole in thinking, emotions, desires, and actions. I declare that my peace within is fully restored to my mind, body, soul, and spirit. Lord, heal and remove everything that is causing stress, grief, and sorrow in my life. Let your peace reign in my

family, at work, and everything I lay my hands. In Jesus name, Amen."

Traci Steele

Day 23

***"Be kind and compassionate to one another, forgiving each other, just as in Christ God forgave you."* (Ephesians 4:32)**

Your goal on this spiritual journey is to try to be like Christ. We all know that is not an easy task. He forgave us, which means we can forgive ourselves and others. This is a powerful truth. When someone hurts us, the natural human reactions can be anger, disappointment, bitterness, or even revenge. We often protect ourselves by drawing away from others who could potentially hurt you hence you build up a wall. Your defense mechanism is built up, and you keep everyone at arm's length. In the case of a relationship, this may lead to isolation from everyone or never giving your full 100% in future relationships. For me, one of the hardest things to do is forgive someone who has hurt me. After all, doesn't forgiving mean I'm giving up, giving in, or letting them win? Does it mean I'm over it? That the hurt they caused doesn't matter anymore? In actuality, forgiving is not for the other person. Until you can forgive, you continue to carry around hurt, anger, hate, and sorrow. All deep emotions that affect your body, the way you see yourself, the way you see others, and the way you see the world. Not forgiving can keep you stuck in all of these emotions. Today, ask God to release these deep seeded feelings and aid you on your path to forgiveness.

Today's Prayer:

"Father God, my deepest desire is to know You more and to experience Your love fully. I understand the importance of forgiveness as I forgive others for any misguided words or action. Your love can open my eyes and heart to the realization that no one except me owns my happiness and no one can take my joy from me. I forgive myself for holding on to emotions or actions that are not of You. I release it to You today. Let this be a new beginning. Releasing the past and embracing forgiveness, I am refreshed and renewed through Your glory and feel uplifted in Your spirit, Amen."

Day 24

"In everything give thanks, for this is the will of God in Christ Jesus concerning you."
(1 Thessalonians 5:18 KJV)

During the low times of my life, I have always used gratitude to pull me back to a place of balance. Thinking about the things in my life that I have to be grateful for always lifts me up out of my "why me" attitude. This kind of mentality can carry me down into depression and make me feel as if I'm drowning. Gratitude can bring to mind the miracles in your life. It can remind you of all of the beautiful people that love and support you. It puts a smile on your face when you focus on your blessings instead of your trials. Being thankful can honestly change your entire mood. Today, after your daily prayer, I want you to write down five things that bring you joy. Then I want you to start a gratitude journal. Include five things in your journal that you are grateful for each day. What a wonderful way to start the day.

Today's Prayer:

"Lord, I DECLARE I am grateful for who God is in my life and for what he has done. I will not take for granted the people, the opportunities, the favor and blessings. I will focus on my blessing and not my troubles. I will see each day as a gift from God. My heart will overflow with praise and gratitude for all of his goodness. Lord, continue to be my refuge and my rock. Refresh me with your anointing. In Jesus name, I pray, Amen."

Day 25

"But seek first the kingdom of God and his righteousness, and all these things will be added to you." (Matthew 6:33)

At this point, anyone who is doing this cleanse ultimately wants a healthy relationship or marriage. But often people are not taking the right steps to gain the proper connection. You desire marriage or a boyfriend more than you desire to know God. To make it worse, when God doesn't send you a soulmate, you get offended. You start to question God. He has the power why doesn't He send me my significant other? You get angry, cry, scream, and yell out, "Where is he, Lord?" Without knowing, you stop trusting in Him. You cease to acknowledge him or his authority over your life.

When in actuality you were supposed to seek God before you seek a partner. Today, ask God to help you in your spiritual growth.

Today's Prayer:

"Father God, I seek your love and guidance. I choose to put you first. I pray that I grow closer to you with each passing day and that I will feel you in every area of my life. Lord be in my thoughts, words, and deeds. I let go and place you in control of all things. In Jesus name, Amen."

Day 26

"Flee from sexual immorality. All other sins a person commits are outside the body, but whoever sins sexually, sins against their own body." (1 Corinthians 6:18 NIV)

Let's talk about sex! I am the last person on the planet who should run around telling people not to have sex because I've had my share of thot moments. But I will say this; I touched on the bond that happens during sex, so you probably know where I'm going with this. I am not trying to convince you to save sex for marriage. I can't do that, only God can. But I can tell you valid reasons to wait. There are tons of practical, common sense reasons to wait that have significant consequences. Some consequences include: dealing with the possibility of pregnancy, acquiring or sharing a sexually transmitted disease, and the most underrated but possibly most impacting are the emotional ties that come with sex. Your bonding with men who are not right for you. That has to stop. Even though the bible says sex before marriage is a sin; I mean sex with the wrong person is insane. Because eventually, they will drive your ass crazy. So today, ask God to give you the strength to wait for the man he has created for you.

Today's Prayer:

"Heavenly Father, as my creator You know me even better than I know myself. Patience does not come easy for me, but I am filled with gratitude and praise knowing that You will sustain me. I'm sorry for rushing ahead when Your hand has not opened the door. Lord, I know You have someone special for me because You have a perfect plan. So, I trust You, and I will wait on You."

Traci Steele

Day 27

***"Do not be misled: Bad company corrupts good character."* (1 Corinthians 15:33 NIV)**

Take a moment and look at your friends. Are they helping you to be a better person? Are they lifting your spirit and supporting your growth? Are they positive people who care about your well-being? Believe it or not, friendships are vital in life. Friends are our family outside the closed walls of the home. They have an enormous contribution in making us who we are as individuals. Their importance in life is tremendous; so, you want to make sure you surround yourself with people who only want to see you flourish, add value to your life, and vice versa.

Today's prayer:

"Heavenly Father, please help me to love my friends with kindness, humility, and honesty. Place people in my life who help me rather than criticize and condemn me. Help them to forgive my shortcomings as I am not perfect. Bless our friendship so that we can all support each other as we follow Your path and Your word together. In Jesus name, we pray, Amen."

Day 28

"For I know the plans I have for you, plans to prosper you and not to harm you, plans to give you hope and a future."

(Jeremiah 29:11, NIV)

I'm writing this book every day while I am on this cleanse and I have noticed today, within the last 28 days, I have focused less on a relationship and marriage and more on myself and career. Which is so crazy to me because I used to pray every single day for a husband, and in the last 28 days I haven't asked once, "where is he?" The cleanse genuinely helped me focus on me, my goals, career, and future. I hope you feel the same way. For 28 days consistently, you have been seeking peace and prosperity as well as a better connection with your Lord and Savior. Today, ask God to continue to protect you and for you to continue to prosper.

Today's Prayer:

"Father God, it is your desire for me to prosper in all that I do. I speak forth promotions, business ideas, and divine connections. Thank you for helping me to know myself and guiding me towards Your will. I know that Your love and light surround me and Your power protect me. In Jesus name, Amen."

Day 29

"Is anyone among you in trouble? Let them pray. Is anyone happy? Let them sing songs of praise." (James 5:13)

Prayer is the way in which we communicate with God. He wants to get to know us better. The verses in this book are meant to encourage your daily walk with Christ and help you experience the power of prayer! We are almost done with this cleanse, and I want to stress the importance of you praying daily, even after this cleanse is over. With prayer you are acknowledging God and accepting Him as your Christ and Savior. Be confident that God knows and wants what is best for you. Ask that He will be done in all we seek from Him. Then, thank Him for it, even though it hasn't happened yet.

Today's Prayer:

"Lord, I pray that I may realize my authority in prayer. Teach me to pray with Your strength and power. I want to work together with You in prayer to determine my future. I want to pray with authority for my people. I desire to pray powerful breakthrough prayers that move Your hand to action. Teach me to come to You daily and pray faith-filled prayers for my needs and the need of those around me, Amen."

Day 30

You made it, Congratulations! 30 Days of prayer and reflections! You are ready to now face the world with a clear mind and closer relationship to God through your prayers. My goal with writing this book was for you to build up your self-esteem and find the strength and courage to let the wrong man go to make room for the right man. Not only that, I wanted you to feel God, know Him, trust in Him more than ever. Then you'll be able to see the amazing things He can do in your life when you trust Him and you're obedient to God. I feel a massive sense of accomplishment, not just because I wrote a book in 30 days, but I was able to reach millions of people with Gods word. That brings me more joy then you will ever imagine. Thank you for taking this journey with me. I feel like I was there praying with you every day.

Today I want you to say this prayer:

"I give thanks to God for this day, in which my dream will flourish, my plans will succeed, my destiny will be assured, and the desires of my heart will be granted in Jesus name, Amen."

ABOUT THE AUTHOR

Traci Steele is a TV and Radio Personality. She is an entrepreneur, fashionista, renowned celebrity DJ, and now an author. Traci was born and raised in Bronx, New York and after joining the United States Air Force, she moved to Virginia where she was stationed at Langley Air Force Base. With an honorable career in the military, Traci gained the confidence needed as a woman that led her to become one of the most talented and influential DJ's in the 21st Century.

A brief stint at Hampton University radio station 88.1 FM soon evolved and elevated Traci into an On-Air Personality on HOT 102.1 FM in Virginia Beach,

VA; then she moved to the music mecca Atlanta, GA where she advanced her career in radio and television. Traci's notoriety garnered a touring opportunity with some of the most elite names in the music industry: Musiq Soulchild, Jazmine Sullivan, and Ne-Yo to name a few. Some of America's most distinguished and respected Corporate Brands (Coca~Cola, Essence, BET, SWAC, Cricket Wireless, Budweiser, Miller Coors, and a host of others) have utilized Traci to Host/DJ many of their premiere events.

With a unique personality and a witty sense of humor, Traci's charisma transcended into numerous television appearances. You've seen her on Bounce TV's Show (Off The Chain), BET's Show (106 & Park), VH1's Show (Love & Hip Hop - Season 2), ABC's

Good Morning America, WeTv Millionaire Matchmaker & a late night talk show, Donnie After Dark on TV One. A phenomenal business woman with a passion for enhancing the lives of others, Traci has served as Brand Ambassador for AIDS Alabama and she hosted an Annual Charity Event Steele Pretty Rocks to accumulate funding for nonprofit organizations. Learn more about Traci by logging on to TraciSteele.com. Follow her on all social media platforms @TraciSteele and check out her clothing line on SteelePretty.com.

Traci Steele

Made in the USA
Middletown, DE
22 April 2018